Contents

KT-226-327

What are grasshoppers?

Grasshoppers are **insects**. They have six legs. There are many different types in the world.

BUG BOOKS

Grasshopper

Karen Hartley, Chris Macro and Philip Taylor

www.heinemann.co.uk/library
Visit our website to find out more information about Heinemann Library books.

To order:
 Phone 44 (0) 1865 888066
 Send a fax to 44 (0) 1865 314091
Visit the Heinemann Bookshop at www.heinemann.co.uk/library to browse our catalogue and order online.

First published in Great Britain by Heinemann Library, Halley Court, Jordan Hill, Oxford OX2 8EJ, part of Harcourt Education.
Heinemann is a registered trademark of Harcourt Education Ltd.

Editorial: Clare Lewis and Katie Shepherd
Design: Ron Kamen, Michelle Lisseter and Bridge Creative Services Limited
Illustrations: Alan Fraser at Pennant Illustration
Picture Research: Maria Joannou
Production: Helen McCreath

Printed and bound in China by South China Printers

13 digit ISBN 978 0 431 01842 3 (hardback)
10 09 08 07 06
10 9 8 7 6 5 4 3 2 1

13 digit ISBN 978 0 431 01910 9 (paperback)
11 10 09 08 07
10 9 8 7 6 5 4 3 2 1

British Library Cataloguing in Publication Data
Hartley, Karen
Bug Books: Grasshopper - 2nd Edition
595.7'26
A full catalogue record for this book is available from the British Library.

Acknowledgements
The publishers would like to thank the following for permission to reproduce photographs:
Ardea: p**8**, J Daniels p**17**, P Goetgheluck pp**5**, **11**, **13**, **14**, **24**, J Mason p**10**; Bruce Coleman Limited: J Burton p**25**, W Cheng Ward p**12**, M Fogden p**7**, H Reinhard p**20**, K Taylor pp**6**, **26**; Corbis: N J Dennis p**21**; Garden and Wildlife Matters: p**27**; Getty Images/The Image Bank: M Mead p**16**; Trevor Clifford: pp**28**, **29**; NHPA: S Dalton pp**18**, **21**, **22**, H and V Ingen p**15**; Okapia: P Clay p**23**, M Wendler p**4**; Oxford Scientific Films: L Crowhurst p**9**.

Cover photograph reproduced with permission of Getty Images/The Image Bank.

The publishers would like to thank Nancy Harris for her assistance in the preparation of this book.

Any words appearing in the text in bold, **like this**, are explained in the Glossary

Some grasshoppers are called **crickets**. Some large grasshoppers are called **locusts**.

5

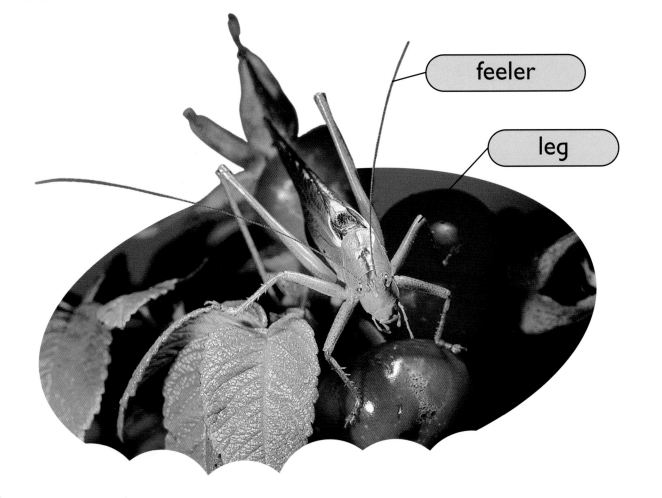

feeler

leg

Grasshoppers have long bodies. They
have four long wings and large eyes.
They have two **feelers** on their heads.
The two back legs of a grasshopper
are much longer than the other four.

Grasshoppers have very hard skin which is green or brown. This one is the same colour as the plants it lives on.

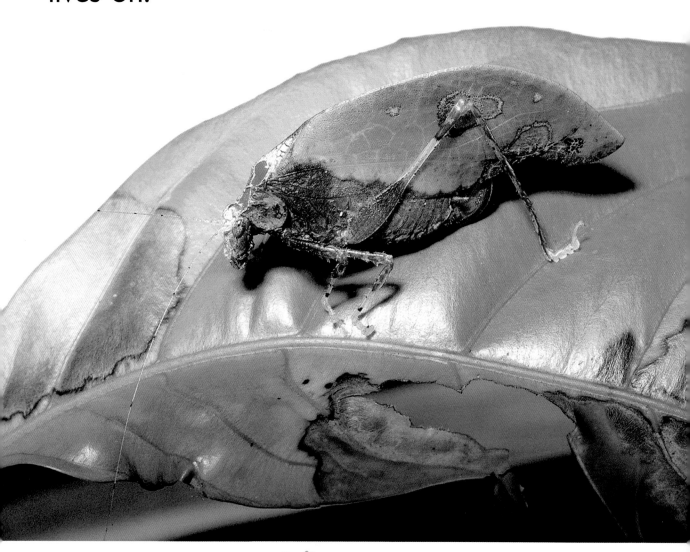

Some grasshoppers are much bigger than others. Many grasshoppers are about as long as your little finger.

female

male

Female grasshoppers are a bit longer than the **males**. Apart from the difference in size, the males and females look alike.

How are grasshoppers born?

The **female** grasshopper lays about 100 eggs in late summer. She covers them with a sticky liquid. This goes hard and protects them.

Young grasshoppers **hatch** out of the eggs in spring. They are very small. They look like **adults** without proper wings.

How do grasshoppers grow?

Grasshoppers grow very quickly.
When they get too big, the skin splits.
The grasshopper crawls out. A new skin
has grown underneath the old one.
This is called **moulting**.

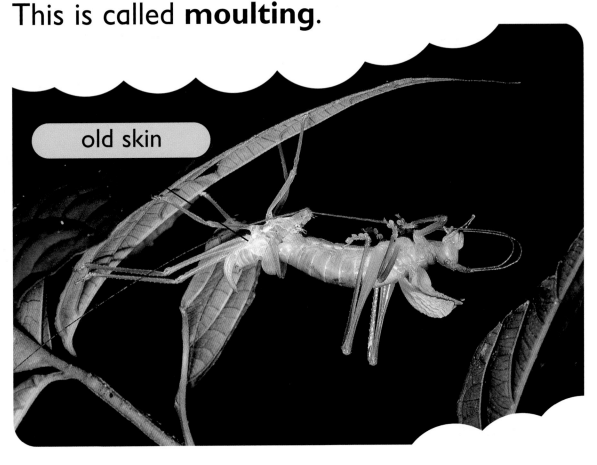

old skin

Grasshoppers moult four to six times before they are grown up. When they are bigger the new skins have wings.

What do grasshoppers eat?

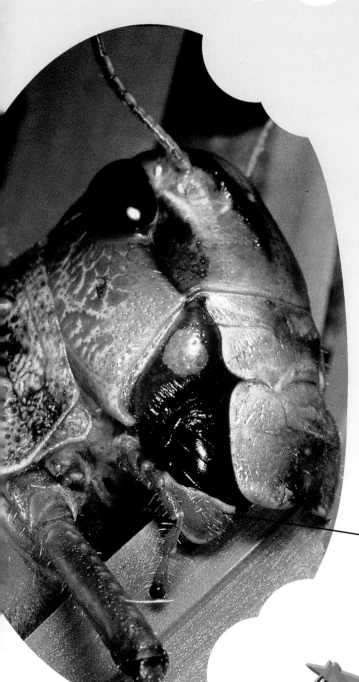

Grasshoppers have strong jaws called **mandibles**. They use them to cut and chew the grass and leaves that they eat. Some crickets eat caterpillars, snails and worms.

mandibles

Locusts are large grasshoppers. They live in big groups called **swarms**. They can eat fields of crops in a short time.

Which animals eat grasshoppers?

Most grasshoppers are attacked when they are still in the egg, or when they are very young. Spiders eat them if they land on their webs. Birds, snakes and lizards also eat grasshoppers.

Frogs and newts catch grasshoppers
with their long tongues.

How do grasshoppers move?

Grasshoppers usually move by jumping. They have very long back legs to give a strong push off the ground. They can jump very high.

All grasshoppers have large wings, but only **locusts** are good at flying.

Where do grasshoppers live?

Grasshoppers live in nearly every country. Most grasshoppers live in thick grassland or woodland.

Some grasshoppers live in houses and some live under the ground. Others live in sand dunes and some live on cliffs.

How long do grasshoppers live?

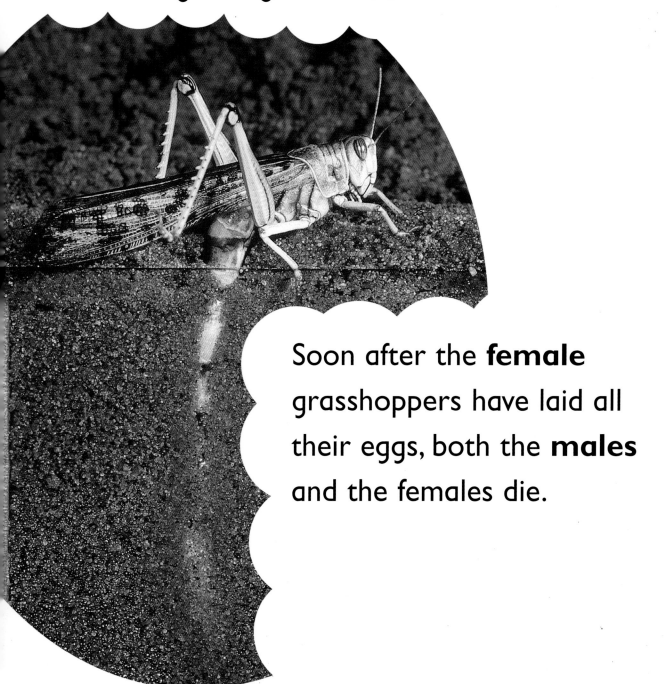

Soon after the **female** grasshoppers have laid all their eggs, both the **males** and the females die.

Grasshoppers cannot live through
a cold winter but the eggs survive.
They **hatch** in the spring.

eggs

How are grasshoppers special?

Male grasshoppers can make a singing noise. They rub the bumps on their back legs along the hard edges of their wings to make the noise.

Male grasshoppers sing to attract females.

Male grasshoppers spend a lot of time on grass stalks. Their singing can last all day and all night.

Each type of grasshopper has a different song. The **females** know which is the right song for them.

Thinking about grasshoppers

These two children are looking for grasshoppers. They can hear them in the grass. They want to watch what the grasshoppers do for a day or two.

They have brought a plastic tank with them. What will they need to put into the tank so the grasshoppers can live there? Where would be the best place to put the tank?

Bug map

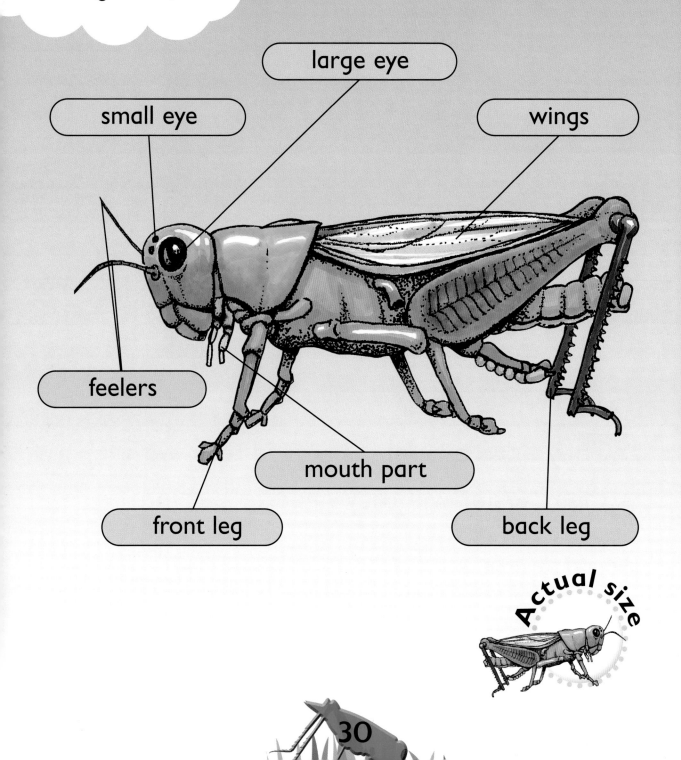

large eye

small eye

wings

feelers

mouth part

front leg

back leg

Actual size

30

Glossary

adult a grown-up

cricket a type of grasshopper with very long feelers

feelers thin growths from the head of an insect that help the insect to know what is around it

female a girl

hatch to come out of an egg

insect a small animal with six legs

locust type of large grasshopper that usually lives in hot countries

male a boy

mandibles parts of the mouths of insects, used for biting and chewing

moulting when a grasshopper grows too big for its skin, it grows a new one and slides out of the old one

swarm a large group of many, many insects

Index

More books to read

Grasshoppers Up Close, Greg Pyers (Raintree, 2005)